How To Manage Your Money

An All Inclusive, Step By Step Guide To Saving Money,
Managing Your Budget, And Managing Your Money,
Designed For Both Beginners And Professionals, And A
Practical Guide To Saving For Debts And Building Wealth

Benton Vasquez

TABLE OF CONTENT

For Eight Reasons You Make The Deposits You Do

First of all, you wish to safeguard a reputation.

You spend the money you do, first and foremost, to safeguard the reputation you have worked so hard to establish. It's not bad to have a "rich image"—faking one is! I understand that you boarded the moving train. Why did I say that? I said it since a lot of individuals in today's world live like that. It goes by the straightforward term "packaging." I don't mind that you boarded the train since it was evident that you were unable to handle the pressure. You submitted to the adage, "join them if you can't beat them."

As I previously stated, pretending to have a wealthy appearance is problematic. I explained to you in the last chapter that every action has an impact, both positive and negative, regardless of the situation in which it was taken (knowing or unconsciously). Investing in image protection is not an exemption. Maintaining an affluent lifestyle does not stress the wealthy; rather, it is the antithesis of living a packaged life, which may include you.

A packaged lifestyle uses all available tricks to mimic the actual one. People who lead this kind of lifestyle have the idea that someone is someone they are not. 'I'm not who you believe I am,' is the fundamental idea. Instead, I am who I believe you to be.

The primary problem with excessive spending starts here because you'll have to sacrifice the realities of your actual income in order to acquire everything that will make you appear like the persona you're portraying. It's been said that you have to learn to live within your means if you want to avoid financial crises in the future.

This is acknowledged by the business community as well, as seen by the proverb, "When expenses exceed income, an organization experiences deficit." Do you understand now why you are unable to hold onto money? For no other reason than to preserve your reputation, you go beyond your means.

It begs the question, why pretend when it can be real? Did you not hear that Rome wasn't constructed in a single day? If you embrace the real world and give up your fantasy lifestyle, your financial situation will drastically improve. Living a packaged life has the risk of being too addicted to quit, and most of the time, its consequences, including guilt, make quitting such a life difficult.

This book was written to assist you in shifting to a more superior mindset—not to stroke your ego. Therefore, please do so if facing the embarrassment is necessary to put things right. Shame doesn't kill, so if using it to get out of your excessive spending disaster is your only option, go ahead and take it. Don't defend an external image that is destroying your inner self. What's your call, then? Continue living your life to please others, spending everything you own to accept your actual situation and begin living within your means. Without hesitation, I would always go with the latter. You ought to follow suit as well!

The Foundations Of Budgeting And Accounting

JO went to his basement after he got home that evening and began going through some old filing cabinets that held his store's historical documents. A lot of bookkeeping was required, including the use of spreadsheets, accounts payable, accounts receivable, and receipts. He knew accounting required more dedication than he felt Sally realized because he had done it for his store.

He wasn't all that excited about the notion the following day.

"You don't seem very excited," said SALLY.

"Who gets excited about accounting?" asked JO.

SALLY: "I think you'll succeed; I don't think you realize how much software has evolved. Before we proceed to the next phase, which is learning the fundamentals of personal accounting and budgeting, let's get you past the outdated perspective on accounting.

Step Four:

Essentials of Personal Budgeting and Accounting

Our understanding of where our money goes will improve with more up-to-date and precise budget data. Our budget data might be one of the most significant things to show us where we can make adjustments to our funds if we want to save money or budget for a big buy.

Keeping track of and allocating funds for our finances.

"Accounting" and "budgeting" are arguably the two most boring words in the English language. But we approach them with far more fear than is necessary, and we fail to see how crucial they are to keeping our finances in good shape. Three duties come to mind when we think of our accounting and budgeting: accounting, decision-making, and budgeting.

Accounting's basic goal is to monitor our earnings and outlays over a given period. One way to conceptualize this more simply is as "gathering financial data."

For instance, we would need to compile our financial data for at least a month if we wanted to determine how much we were spending each month in our grey spending area.

Choices

We have to decide what to do with the information we have. Let's take an example where we decide we want to go to a movie but discover there isn't enough money in our bank account. We have the option of choosing not to see the film or finding another way to pay for it.

Setting a budget

All it takes to create a budget is deciding how much money to allocate to various areas of our lives. It is the steps we take as a consequence of the judgments we have made and the information we have gathered.

Budgeting is when we start making cuts in other areas of our spending to make up for things like when we want to buy a new car but don't have enough money.

Chapter 2: AN APPROACH TO THE RAT RACE

the much-maligned "rat race." All of us have heard the term before, and a lot of us can relate to it too much. It's the routine of putting in long hours at a job that depletes your spirit and leaves you feeling dissatisfied, all while earning little to no financial independence. It's the sensation of always needing to earn more money to support the way of life you've become accustomed to but never having enough time or money to really escape the never-ending cycle of work and consumerism. Indeed, those who compete in the rat race tend to spend more money than they make.

Furthermore, let's be honest: we've all been there. Everybody has had a job when they felt like they were working endlessly to meet the demands of everyday life or like they were just spinning their wheels. Everybody has experienced the urge to work harder, spend more money, and keep up with the Joneses—even if doing so means compromising their happiness and well-beingwellbeing.

The rat race is not a death sentence, yet here's the thing. It's not some unavoidable fate that we must all endure till we retire. It's a way of thinking about money and employment that keeps us mired in a fear-based and scarce cycle. Lack of autonomy and control over one's time and resources are hallmarks of the rat race.

Rather than working towards their own goals and objectives, many people feel as though they are working only to keep up with their expenses and pay the bills.

The traditional career path and 9–5 occupations are frequently linked to the "rat race," wherein individuals are expected to work long hours in exchange for a consistent salary and the possibility of development. The rat race, however, can also occur in other types of employment, such as gig or freelance labor, where individuals may experience pressure to take on as much work as they can in order to survive.

People who are in the rat race often feel like they are living on a treadmill and find it difficult to. But because they need to make a living and provide for their families, a lot of people believe that they are forced to enter the rat race.

It takes a mental change and a dedication to achieving financial independence and personal fulfillment to escape the rat race. In actuality, some people have managed to escape the rat race and discover rich, satisfying lives without compromising their time or sanity.

Consider what really matters to you instead of pursuing more material possessions and money all the time. Create a business or career that is in line with your interests and values, and look for ways to make money without having to give up your time. Make a budget that will not only let you spend every penny you make but also allow you to invest and save for the future.

It won't be simple, and it won't happen overnight. But you can escape the rat race and design a life that is genuinely worthwhile if you have a little bravery, imagination, and perseverance.

It takes dedication to seek financial freedom through investments and alternate sources of income in order to escape the rat race. This could entail taking chances, going after entrepreneurship, or making investments in things that yield passive income. Financial freedom can be attained by taking charge of your finances and pursuing a more autonomous, rewarding lifestyle in place of the corporate world.

✏️The significance of identifying the traps and the rat race

A vital first step in reaching financial freedom and building a more satisfying life is realizing the traps of the rat race. It's crucial to realize that the rat race may manifest itself in a variety of contexts, not only in typical 9–5 occupations but also in freelance or gig-based employment, where the pressure to take on more work in order to increase revenue can result in fatigue and burnout.

It's critical to recognize the telltale indications of the rat race, which include living paycheck to paycheck even with a respectable income, feeling overburdened by work all the time, and having trouble juggling work and personal obligations. It's about realizing that we might become caught in a cycle of work and consumption if we pursue money and material items incessantly without taking into account our total well-being and personal fulfillment.

We can begin taking action to escape the rat race as soon as we are aware of its traps. This could entail reevaluating our priorities and beliefs, establishing specific financial objectives, putting together a budget and savings strategy, and looking into alternate forms of income that fit with our hobbies and passions. It might also entail developing appropriate boundaries and the ability to say no in order to prevent burnout from coming from taking on too much work.

A Summary of One's Financial Situation

A study found that more than 75% of Americans don't fully understand basic financial concepts. It's much worse when it comes to women. Over 80% of women lack financial literacy.

Our financial future seems to be made up of a million colorful soap bubbles when we graduate. One involves Mr. or Mrs.'s future, our kids and all of their life experiences, and perhaps a third that we would like to carry on with. A fourth might be the ideal spot. Every dream we have is a component of our financial situation. We can envision ourselves utilizing credit to reach any or all of our objectives. These days, it is how economies grow, and everyone is urged to do it.

Regretfully, somewhere along the line, the idea of paying for the use of that money got muddy. Not only is there money involved, but also a sequence of payments, interest rates, and credit card benefits, all adding up to a sum of money that exceeds the original purchase price. We owe money. We owe money.

Every stage of your family life may present different challenges and opportunities. Planning is one of the most crucial things you can do to be ready for the next big event in your life. Whether you are getting married or having a kid, it is crucial to be ready for the financial toll that these events will take on your life. It's crucial to be adaptable because starting a family could be one of the biggest financial decisions you make. Enhancing family budgeting can facilitate the shift and create long-term financial security.

What Is Personal Finance, in Your Opinion?

The planning and administration of one's financial activities, including income generating, spending, saving, investing, and security, is known as personal finance. A budget or financial plan can provide an overview of the personal money management process. This chapter examines the most prevalent and significant facets of personal financial management.

Personal Finance Topics

To fully grasp the subject, we will focus on dissecting the essential components of personal finance in this chapter and going into further detail about each one.

The primary facets of personal finance are income, expenses, savings, and security, as will be discussed below. We'll go into more detail about each of these elements below.

Revenue

An individual's income is the source of cash flow that they receive and utilize to sustain themselves and their family. This marks the beginning of our financial planning phase.

The following are typical sources of income: pensions, wages, dividends, bonuses, and salaries.

A person can spend, save, or invest the money they get from any of these sources of income. In this context, revenue can be viewed as the starting point of our personal finance road plan. Every expense falls into two categories: credit (payable for borrowed money) and cash (payable for cash on hand). The majority of citizens spend the majority of their wealth.

Rent, taxes, food, credit card payments, mortgage payments, entertainment, and travel are common sources of expenditure. These costs take away from an individual's ability to save and invest money. A person has a deficit if their expenses are more than their income. People typically keep an eye on their discretionary spending rather than their profits, despite the fact that managing spending is just as important as generating income. Maintaining sound spending practices is essential to handling personal finances well.

Conserving

Savings is the act of setting aside extra money for future purchases or investments. A person may choose to save or invest any extra revenue that arises from their expenditures over their income. One important area of personal finance is savings management.

Typical deposits consist of • Hard currency • Bank account for savings • Bank account for checking

Keeping investments helps most people manage their cash flow and the short-term difference between their income and expenses. However, an excessive amount of savings could be considered insufficient as it yields minimal to no returns on investments.

Resolving Problems

The ability to solve problems gives you the power to overcome obstacles, exercise critical thought, and come up with novel solutions.

"You can confidently and creatively negotiate life's curveballs if you have mastered the art of effective problem solving."

Problem-solving: What Is It?

Consider difficulties as jigsaw pieces that need to be put together and view life as a puzzle. The process of assessing a situation, recognizing barriers or difficulties, and coming up with solutions is known as problem-solving. It involves deciphering complicated problems and coming up with answers by applying your intelligence, inventiveness, and ingenuity. Analytical reasoning, brainstorming, and a willingness to try out different solutions are all necessary for effective issue-solving.

How to Address Issues Head-on

1. Defining the Issue and Exposing the Challenge: To begin with, precisely identify the issue you're dealing with. Dissect it into its constituent parts and identify the underlying causes. If you're having trouble managing your time, for example, pinpoint the precise areas that you're having trouble with.

2. Collect Information - Laying the Groundwork: Prior to tackling problems, compile pertinent data and insights. Do your homework, ask around, and, if needed, consult specialists. If you're attempting to change the way you study, learn about the various methods and how successful they are.

3. Provide Solutions - Unveiling Originality: List as many options as you can, regardless of how strange they look. Give yourself permission to explore a variety of ideas and think beyond the box. For example, if you struggle to maintain organization, you might want to think about employing digital tools, making physical

organizers, or putting in place reminder mechanisms.

4. Evaluate Options - Weighing the Pros and Cons: Consider the viability, efficacy, and possible results of each possible option. Think about the long- and short-term effects. When choosing how to balance your classes and part-time jobs, weigh the benefits and drawbacks of various scheduling strategies.

5. Choosing the Best Option and Making the Decision: Select the course of action that best fits your objectives, principles, and available means. Have faith in your judgment and keep in mind that there may not always be a single "best" option; sometimes, the most appropriate one is what matters.

6. Put the Solution Into Practice - Acting: Implement the solution that you have selected. Make a plan, set aside funds, then go forward with putting it into action. Engaging in meaningful discussions and practicing active listening are good places to start when trying to improve your communication abilities.

7. Monitor and Adjust - Navigating the Path: Keep an eye on the outcomes of your solution at all times, and be ready to make modifications as necessary. keep a frequent record of your progress and adjust your training regimen in response to your successes and setbacks.

The Advantages of Solving Problems

1. Sharper Minds - Enhanced Critical Thinking: Solving problems will hone your analytical and

critical thinking abilities. You get adept at breaking down complicated problems, analyzing data, and coming to wise judgments.

2. Enhanced Creativity - Unlocking Innovation: Solving problems fosters your capacity for original thought. It inspires you to investigate novel ideas and come up with original answers.

3. Confidence Building - Promoting Self-Assuredness: You get confidence when you solve difficulties effectively. Your resilience and self-belief are strengthened by every obstacle you overcome.

4. Adaptability - Thriving in Change: Solving problems gives you the flexibility to deal with ambiguity and modify your approach when confronted with novel circumstances.

5. Better Decision Making: Orienting Your Selections: Making decisions and addressing problems are related. You improve your capacity to make decisions that are consistent with your values and aspirations as you gain expertise in solving problems.

6. Innovation and Resourcefulness - Becoming a Trailblazer: People who are good at solving problems go on to become trailblazers and innovators. They are skilled at coming up with novel solutions to problems and bringing about constructive change.

7. Personal Growth - Unveiling Your Potential: Solving problems is a path towards personal development and self-awareness. Every issue you

resolve advances your personal growth and gives you useful life skills.

Your beacon of light in the maze of possibilities and problems is problem-solving. This ability enables you to solve puzzles, overcome obstacles, and come up with creative solutions. The ability to solve problems effectively is your compass, whether you're dealing with personal issues, overcoming academic obstacles, or pursuing lofty objectives. Utilize this chapter as a resource to help you develop into a quick thinker, an inventive problem solver, and a self-assured problem solver who is prepared to take on any issue life throws at you.

ANALYSING THE VISION

While many employees long to work for themselves, many are afraid of what would happen to their businesses if they become owners. If you're one of those folks, I would like to suggest that you would be well to become an exceptional representative first! I worked as an employee for many years, and I was always found to be an excellent representative.

My business manager consistently gave me excellent ratings. I can honestly tell you that after seeing the employee mindset summary, I didn't have those attitudes. I was a fantastic representative! You can begin now if you find yourself needing to be independent one day in order to pursue your business goals. Treat your job as though you own the company where you are employed.

Having that proprietorship spirit will make you more productive at work and better equipped for the day you can pursue your venture. It is possible to conduct business while working. Possessing this soul will give you the drive to pursue your own goals when you're not working for your boss. Be truthful with yourself about your strengths and weaknesses, and then allocate time and work accordingly. It may be beneficial to start with the activities you enjoy the most because they will likely require more effort, and you will undoubtedly finish more engaging tasks.

Plan for events and adhere to the allotted time - Inefficient meetings that end late are a major source of inefficiency.

Record all important information, such as the date, time, and participants. When taking notes, organize and rearrange the items. This could prevent later amazing speculation. In the event of failure, archive.

Learn how to accomplish your tasks with new and improved tools, and take some time to become even more proficient with the ones you already have.

Seek guidance from a mentor or coach,enroll in a course on authoritative procedures, efficient business correspondence, and time management. Take pauses. When you're feeling overwhelmed, this could seem to be conflicting. In either case, "time to get down to business" designates the moment when being focused and clear becomes much more critical. Making mistakes is easy, especially when you're feeling overwhelmed. Planned breaks into your day are actually essential. Yes, even a quick walk around the building can help you decompress and reduce stress, which is beneficial.

Determine the best way to listen to customers. Observe and learn from the family members you work with since they consistently display the traits you'll need to maintain your company persona, such as paying attention to customers.

Take Note of What People Desire

Talk about listening is very common these days. One of the most important skills you can learn is how to listen. If you can actually stop and listen to your customers, you will be able to move your firm towards success.

Paying attention to what clients need and want requires concentration. If you have your own business, you must practice the art of giving someone your whole attention. It is insufficient to address client inquiries. You have to be able to anticipate their needs. Taking care of your clients is closely related to positioning your business to be the answer to their requirements, ideally before they even ask.

Additionally, listening involves interacting with your clients. This includes spending real time and effort with them, learning about topics that are meaningful to them, reading books and publications that are written with them in mind, and becoming an authority on the subjects that matter to them.

The ideal client should be present in your business. This is how you should envision your perfect client. This is the kind of customer you need to draw in, and the more of them that meet the ideal, the better. Consequently, it follows that this is the type of client you ought to be targeting. A customer is someone who has purchased from you or the company you work for, but they can also purchase in the future. Customers, prospects, and the general public should all be treated with the same respect. In either case, you should focus your attention on the clients who are most in need of your services.

It is possible and desirable to listen anywhere. That being said, you can use particular tools and methods to improve your tuning in. Disconnected, you ought to be in charge of customer research and just go out and talk to people. Attend career fairs and events that your ideal clients are also attending. Create one if there aren't already any in your area.

You should consider performing a couple of talking presentations as your level of expertise grows. This is a fantastic way to meet new people and ask them to tell you about the problems they are facing. There are many opportunities on the internet. With the help of Twitter Search, you can tune in on Twitter. Google Alerts allows you to track terms and phrases online.

Events are fantastic places to tune in. Furthermore, a blog or digital broadcast can be used to provide original listening posts. Yes, this is about you talking, but it will also motivate you to research and learn more about your clientele. You can also read comments and stimulate discussion.

Pay attention to what clients are saying when they speak. If your true goal is to find out where your ideal clients congregate—both offline and online—you must be present there as well. Giving your full attention will help you better understand and communicate with your clients. Deals and promotions will be easier since you will be able to place yourself in the direct line of sight between the customer and the need.

Developing a remarkable following can also endear you to the individuals you want to connect with. Everybody enjoys being given attention. Close that loop, put away that profit and loss statement for a moment, and begin exploring the world of your clientele.

Setting A Budget

The cornerstone of personal finance is budgeting. The process of formulating a spending plan is what enables people to manage their finances successfully. One can set spending limits, prioritize costs, and keep track of income and expenses with the use of a budget. One can maximize one's finances and prevent expenditures by making a budget.

Step 1: Calculate Your Income

Finding one's income is the first step in making a budget. Any money received from investments, employment, or other sources is considered income. To construct a realistic budget, it is imperative to have a clear picture of one's income. An individual's income is very predictable if they receive a regular paycheck. Determining income, however, might be more difficult if one has unpredictable revenue, such as from commission-based work or freelancing. Based on prior wages, one can calculate their average monthly income in this situation.

Step 2: Monitor Your Spending

Keeping a tab on one's spending is the next step. Any money spent on bills, groceries, travel, entertainment, and other things is considered an expense. Monitoring spending makes it easier to see where money is going and where savings might be made.

There are various ways to monitor spending, such as:

• Making use of a spreadsheet or budgeting program
• Manually tracking spending and preserving receipts
• Regularly reviewing credit card and bank statements

One can divide their costs into several areas, such as lodging, food, transportation, and entertainment after they have a firm grasp of them.

Step 3: Establish Spending Caps

The next action is to establish spending caps. The amount that can be spent in each area can be calculated based on income and expenses. Setting sensible spending boundaries and abstaining from overspending are crucial.

One approach to establishing spending caps is to apply the 50/30/20 rule. According to this rule, one should set aside 50% of their income for essentials like housing, food, and transportation, 30% for luxuries like shopping and entertainment, and 20% for debt repayment and savings.

Step 4: Set Spending Priorities

Prioritizing spending is crucial after establishing spending caps. Determining which costs are necessary and which ones might be reduced is the process of prioritizing expenses.

Food and housing, for instance, are necessary expenditures that cannot be cut. Shopping and entertainment, on the other hand, are optional costs that can be cut if needed. Making the most of one's finances and avoiding expenditures can be achieved by setting spending priorities.

Step 5: Review and Make Regular Adjustments
Lastly, it's critical to routinely analyze and modify the budget. A new job, an unforeseen expense, or a shift in income are examples of how life circumstances might change. One may make sure the budget is still practical and efficient by routinely examining it.

One may need to change their spending caps or prioritize their expenses if they discover that they are routinely overspending in a specific area. In a similar vein, someone with more money may wish to raise their savings or modify their spending limitations.

The Snowball Technique is the most practical and proven method of repayment.

The killer solution is here, thanks to banking and financial specialists! This goes by the name of the "snowball method" and is primarily intended to assist individuals in becoming accustomed to paying off their debts in a peaceful manner. This is especially beneficial for those who believe that their debt represents the summit of a mountain that they are unable to climb.

"Snowball Method," which could ease the debt trip a bit, according to American Time magazine. Based on data from 2019 and reports to the Federal Bank in New York, the total debt owed by American families was 13.86 trillion dollars. Additionally, estimates published in Time Magazine suggest that about 80% of American adults are in debt, whether it be from credit card debt, mortgages, medical bills, student loans, or payments for their homes, cars, or other properties. You are not alone, so don't worry! What is the snowball method, though, and is it a good fit for your financial plan or for you personally?

The snowball method involves sorting your debts from the smallest balance to the largest balance. However, one type of debt that should not be included in your accounts is your mortgage. It is typically regarded as a "good form of debt" because it is typically backed by an asset (your home), which must ideally be appreciated over time. Matt Frankel, an accredited financial planner and personal finance expert at The Ascent, cites American Time Magazine to explain this concept. According to Frankel, when you've arranged your bills, you can begin utilizing the snowball method, which involves figuring out the minimal interest on each loan and paying off the smallest debt first. The "beginning with this smaller" approach reduces the overall debt by using the least amount of your income to pay off the smallest loan first. It's crucial to pay off the debt in full as soon as you can.

Experts in banking have concluded that this is the case, and subsequent social and analytical research has shown that debt repayment serves as a personal stimulant. The debtor will eventually be able to take a portion of his income, even if it is only a tiny amount, to pay off some of his bills. This will give him motivation, and with time, the amounts you can pay off for your larger debts will occasionally rise.

Sarah Rathner, a credit card expert at NerdWallet, was quoted by "Time" explaining the snowball in more detail and providing an explanation of its workings. it starts small, and over time, it makes a big difference."

Who is the front-runner to win the snowball technique?

According to Frankel and Rathner, individuals with "typical" debt situations—that is, those with relatively small credit card balances, which frequently have higher interest rates, but larger balances on auto or student loans, which typically have lower interest rates—are better suited for the snowball method. It may also be a good option for people who have multiple debts, such as credit card debts, medical bills, student loans, and mortgages—and simply need a place to start. Frankel explains that a suitable candidate for the snowball method would have three credit cards with balances of $200, $500, and $2,000, with an average interest rate of 19.24%. "It also makes sense for people with little small debts to pay off first to build momentum," Frankel says. This individual will settle credit card debt of $200, $500, and $2,000 in addition to the $5,000 vehicle loan sum with an average interest rate of 4.21% and the $20,000 school loan balance with an average interest rate of 4.45%. Prior to starting the repayment of other loans, first.

According to one of Petromaint's senior financial advisers, those who find their debt load to be significant can use the snowball method as a tool to develop good financial habits. "The snowball method is suitable for people who need some behavioural assistance and motivation to get rid of debt," he stated.

According to Frankel and Rathner, the entire situation is connected to these little successes that sustain the momentum. "If you're struggling to stay motivated and win a few gains, it makes you excited to move forward and eliminate debts from your life, the snowball method can help," he stated...

Since we frequently hear the statement, "I am looking for quick victories to continue my positive movements," some experts argue that the snowball method is a good choice from a behavioral perspective. The idea is to find the simplest ways to support oneself and feel like a real badass money manager!

The more little debts are paid off, the more of an incentive there is to keep going and push for larger debt payments.

However, the "snowball" strategy needs to be sustained in order for the individual to learn to follow the prescribed course and become accustomed to the process of setting aside money for repayment. This is because higher-interest debt is prioritized by the Snowball method. After all, smaller debts typically have higher interest rates, whereas larger debts typically have lower interest rates.

Chapter 2: Managing Your Education Loan Repayment

Whether you attended college for two years, four years, or six years or longer, managing your student loans can be challenging.

You might have two or three debts by the end of your academic career. If you go on to graduate school, you might have much more debt. You have some benefits, even though organizing a pile of debt may seem like an uphill battle. If you happen to forget one or two, it's easy to find your federal student loans. Compared to almost any other type of loan, you have more alternatives for temporary payment reprieves, ways to recover financially from late or missing payments, and more possible payment plans to keep your loans affordable within your budget.

Rehab Default

You recently had your mortgage application denied, and you're not sure why. You've had a reliable job for the past five years, you make all of your bill payments on schedule, and you have the necessary down payment in your bank account. You find out you defaulted on a student loan when you question the banker about what went wrong. You're paying your student loan servicers hundreds of dollars each month, so you find it incomprehensible. What took place?

One of your student loans likely went into default because you forgot about it. During my undergraduate years, I did, and 1 in 5 students nationwide did as well. I was making consolidation payments on 15 loans and had forgotten about one. For those of us in this circumstance, the fines were an added burden on top of the seemingly endless interest. This would never have occurred if payments had been made in a planned manner. For this reason, it's critical to maintain organization and timely repayment of your student loans, as well as to act swiftly to avoid default.

Examine your loan statuses using the Personal Student Loan table you made in Chapter 1, "Evaluating Your Student Debt Situation." Take note of any loans that are in default status on your chart, as well as any that you may have forgotten about but could eventually go into default. After all, you can get in touch with your servicer and begin making payments before you have to go through default rehab if you can catch them before the default is formally declared.

The New Beginnings Initiative

For defaulters, the Department of Education established a short-term Fresh Start program. As long as the program is still in place, you can sign up and promptly have the default removed from your credit report. If you go back to school, you can still receive financial aid.

The same programs that are available to people without defaults will also be open to you. It appears as though the default has never happened. Loans held by the Department of Education, FFEL loans, and defaulted direct loans are all eligible. Ineligible loans include those from the Health Education Assistance Loan (HEAL) program, school-held defaulted Perkins loans, direct loans that fall behind after the Covid-19 Payment Pause, and FFEL loans that fall behind after the Covid-19 Payment Pause. To enlist, visit myeddebt.ed.gov. For additional information, call 1-800-621-0315 a call.

The Impact of Defaults on You Not withstanding Fresh Start

You must be aware of the consequences regardless of whether you are in default or just about to default. In this manner, if you haven't already fallen off the cliff, you can get in touch with your servicer to arrange payments. If so, you must get in touch with your guarantee company in order to overcome your default.

The following are potential consequences for defaulting on a student loan, according to data from www.studentaid.ed.gov:

• Your transcripts from college can be withheld.

• Options for student loan repayment programs get fewer in number. • You can lose your eligibility for further federal student loans.

• If a collection agency is assigned to handle, collection costs, and additional charges that will be added to your debt.

• The default may remain on your credit reports for years to come, which could have an impact on your credit ratings.

• The decline in credit ratings may make it more difficult for you to get a mortgage, credit cards, auto loans, or flat rentals.

• Refunds of federal and state income taxes may be deducted and used to settle outstanding student loan balances on delinquent loans.

• Your salary may be garnished in part. they may reject your application. • The government might not hire you.

What happens if you don't have enough cash on hand to pay off your overdue debt right away? Remain optimistic. It is possible to improve your default.

Note: If you were in arrears before the outbreak, salary garnishments are not possible until August 2024. Make payment arrangements as soon as you can, and get in touch with your guarantee company very soon.

Suggestions For Reducing Money On Daily Expenses

In this chapter, we'll go over some practical advice that will help you reduce the cost of your daily spending. Over time, small savings can add up and support debt repayment, wealth accumulation, and financial objectives.

Making a Spending Plan

The first step in saving money on regular spending is to create a budget. You may prioritize your spending and identify your expenses by creating a budget. You can set aside a certain amount of money for each area of expenses, including accommodation, food, entertainment, and other necessities. By doing this, you may stay within your budget and prevent overspending.

Cutting Down on Food Costs

For most households, one of the largest expenses is food. Meal planning, shopping in bulk, and cooking at home are ways to cut costs on food. Additionally, you can purchase generic or store-brand products, hunt for sales and discounts on groceries, and refrain from eating out or getting takeaway too frequently.

Reducing the Cost of Transportation

The cost of transportation might also mount up quickly. By walking, biking, or using public transportation wherever possible, you can reduce your transportation costs. In addition, you may utilize apps to identify the best petrol prices, carpool, and cut down on pointless excursions.

Reducing Electricity Costs

A few easy adjustments can lower the cost of utilities, including gas, water, and electricity. switch off lights and lug electronics when not in use, and take shorter showers. Additionally, you can think about negotiating a lower rate with your existing utility supplier or moving to a less expensive one.

Preventing Needless Memberships and Subscriptions

A lot of people pay for memberships and subscriptions that they neither use nor require.

Any pointless memberships or subscriptions, like magazine subscriptions, streaming services, and gym memberships, can be canceled to save money.

Using Cashback Apps and Coupons

Coupons are available online or in newspapers, and you may use them to save money on apparel, groceries, and other goods. To receive money on your purchases, you can also use cashback applications.

Postponing Gratitude

It can be challenging to postpone gratification, but you can save money by doing so. You can wait to buy something and save up for it rather than buying it right away. This might assist you in controlling your spending and preventing impulsive purchases.

money on regular expenses by implementing these ideas and tactics. It's critical to keep in mind that little that achieving financial success is a process rather than a goal.

WHY IS INVESTMENT ESSENTIAL TO THE GROWTH OF WEALTH?

Investing is important for increasing wealth since it allows you to grow your money over time, avoiding the negative effects of growth and helping you reach your financial goals. A few primary reasons why investment is essential to accumulating wealth are as follows:

1. Beat Expansion: Expansion causes your money's purchasing power to erode over time. It is possible to get returns from investments in stocks, bonds, and real estate that outpace growth. This suggests that your money can maintain or perhaps appreciate over time.

2. Compound Interest: Compounding is one of the most amazing strategies for accumulating wealth. You receive returns on both your initial investment and any profit generated by it at the time of contribution. This compounding effect

has the potential to essentially support your wealth over time.

3. Diversification: Investing allows you to distribute your funds among several assets, reducing the risk involved with holding all of your assets in one location. Enhancement protects your wealth from fluctuations in the market and downturns in the economy.

4. Retirement Planning: Creating a workable retirement savings plan requires investing. It might not be possible to maintain your ideal standard of living in retirement if all you rely on is savings or a fixed income. Investments can help you get past that problem.

5. Wealth Acceleration: Although saving money is essential, it might not be enough to help you reach your financial goals quickly on its own. a traditional savings account, which can accelerate the growth of your wealth.

6. Tax Benefits: Certain investment vehicles provide tax benefits, which are comparable to

tax-conceded growth or, under certain conditions, tax-free withdrawals. With these advantages, you can keep more of your money working for you.

7. Financial Goals: Investing enables you to match your financial goals to your level of risk tolerance. Investing can give you the financial resources needed to turn your ambitions of owning a home, starting a business, or seeing the world into a reality.

8. Emergency Resource: Suitably managing investments can also serve as a source of emergency funds. Although having a separate crisis savings account is essential, investments offer liquidity that can be utilized when needed.

Getting Ready for Change in Chapter 1: "We won't progress if we don't change. If we do not develop, we are not living.

Many fitness regimens include conditioning exercises because they aid in the body's adaptation to novel muscle actions and mental demands. Similar to this, a successful financial fitness program consists of activities that minimize the discomforts related to financial circumstances. Since pursuing improved financial circumstances necessitates constant internal and external change, resistance to such changes is common. The majority of individuals pursuing wealth are averse to change, despite their desire for their lives to be better, as they take comfort in their more stable financial habits.

However, because they are unwilling to put up with temporary misery, they discover financial freedom and fulfillment. Thankfully, by understanding the reasons behind your reluctance and taking proactive steps to make changes, you can gradually alter the deeply ingrained beliefs, attitudes, feelings, and behaviors that have kept you in your current financial circumstance.

THREATS THAT THE IDENTITY FACTOR REPORTS

What you called the Identity Factor—a defense mechanism that preserves a person's sense of self and position in the universe—is one of the reasons for resistance. Changing financial circumstances usually trigger the Identity Factor, which can swiftly put someone in jeopardy. When this occurs, people typically try to postpone making the necessary modifications or revert to their old behaviors in order to preserve their comfortable lifestyle. This is because they fear that the changes will eventually cause them to feel uneasy, scared, and confused. It was uncertain what discomforts would arise from chance. She was establishing responsible financial habits and paying off her debt.

Formulated a plan with the assistance of a credit counselor to pay off her debt, stop using credit cards, and keep better financial records.

After three months of strict program adherence, she was happy with the progress she saw. However, in the fourth month, she began to fall behind on her payments and twice had to borrow money from friends. Out of embarrassment, she stopped maintaining a budget. Still, six months later, she was exactly back where she had been: with greater debt, a propensity to put off taking care of financial concerns, and a hazy grasp of her expenditures.

When Celine first called me, she was angry with herself for standing in the way of her progress.

She realized that her acts were self-protective rather than self-sabotaging after realizing that she had been defending her former identity. She had turned to actions with more foreseeable results in order to defend her identity.

She gradually started to grow and learn how to deal with the discomfort brought on by her altered behaviors, both of which enabled her to stick to her budget.

Significant change can damage someone's sense of self, and it can also have an impact on relationships with peers and family of origin.

People recognize you for who you used to be, so any changes you make to your attitudes or behaviors force them to react to you differently, which causes them to change as well.

Unchangeable friends or family members could try to stand in your way of success, which makes you feel even more miserable because you will believe that you are the only one.

Fortunately, you'll learn that being alone is not inevitable as you get ready for change.

You can revisit past acquaintances and friendships and create new connections with people who reflect your changing identity and who will unavoidably come into your life.

Recognizing the Shifting Dumb People

Beginning a shift to new financial circumstances and behaviors can be challenging at first since the outcome and the journey are both uncertain. If you have ever moved, then you have undoubtedly come across what I call the "moving stupids."

Ailment

Among the symptoms include feelings of being overloaded, confused, lost, and alone, as well as a tendency to misplace items or make poor decisions.

However, the discomforts of moving into a new home gradually subside as your spending habits improve, and you become used to your new surroundings.

By acknowledging the moving stupids as a step towards a better financial situation, you can decrease their duration and move forward. When he reached fifty, he got ready to reassess his relationship with money.

He felt indebted and was embarrassed about his lack of financial literacy despite his desire for financial stability. Agreed to follow a spending plan we developed, stop using his credit cards when he started working with me, and keep track of every dollar he spent.

He whined, "I've got a terrible case of the moving stupids." I'm so afraid I'll make a mistake in my calculations and wind up spending too much.

Also, when I jot down my daily expenses, it feels as though another person is inhabiting my body. This isn't how I normally behave. Told me after a further two weeks that his new behaviors were more natural and that the perplexity and anxiety were gradually going away.

However, he had fleeting epiphanies whenever he implemented a new habit, like setting aside money each pay period.

But he knew the moving stupids were a sign of maturity and would soon stop, so he was ready to go through the experience.

Activities The following actions can help you overcome resistance and get ready for change by raising your level of self-awareness. You practice patience and make progress. To double your efforts, acclimatize to little changes before tackling larger ones.

1. Start a Journal of Prosperity

To assess where you are now and track your progress as you flex your financial muscles, Use it to put down your concerns or reluctance, acknowledge your successes, and underline any questions that spring to mind. You can also use it to convey how you feel about change.

Dating each item facilitates a more comfortable analysis of your findings in the future.

2. Locate a Prosperity Companion

Collaborating with a friend might boost your drive to lessen pain and create a more enjoyable transfer to a new financial situation.

For your experience-sharing sessions, designate a person with whom you feel at ease discussing personal matters on a regular basis—for example, once or twice a week.

During each one, take turns talking about any discomforts you've experienced (such as estrangement or disorientation), noting your progress from the previous session, soliciting criticism if you'd like, and outlining what you'll do before the next one. It's best to avoid criticizing your friend's behavior or giving uninvited advice, as this could lead to conflict.

Rather, encourage your friend by emphasizing their successes. Selecting prosperous friends outside of your relationship is a great choice for couples, particularly if you have emotional conversations about money often. You can work through financial issues with your partner, but confiding in a third party will probably encourage you to be more forthright and honest about issues. People who use the buddy system progress more quickly than those who don't.

Why Is Student Financial Management Important?

Overview
The amount of debt you accrue will depend on how well you have controlled your expenses while still enrolled in classes, even though the majority of students leave with substantial debt and some with less. if you want to avoid having to pay for a significant deficit and save money while you're still in school. Financial management will help you avoid going over your budget while you're still in school, limit your expenditures, and save money from having to pay off your massive debt.

The importance of financial literacy among students.
Financial management is essential, especially for those who lack the funds to pay for their education. Even though students think this is a difficult task, it is beneficial to learn the principles of money management since it could lead to better

opportunities in the future. Here are a few things you should be aware of in order to organize your finances effectively:

• A portion of your earnings from your part-time job or student loan checks should be saved permanently. To follow your passion and get more money, you could try investing a portion of it.

• The current economic cycle should also be kept up to date for students since it pertains to the best times to take out loans. There are times when there is little interest. If you want to know when it's best to invest or reinvest your money, find out when interest rates are high.

• You ought to seize the opportunity when choosing one chance over another. Additionally, you want to be aware of your financial situation, particularly when making decisions about your money, like taking a part-time job and purchasing unnecessary expenditures.

• You also gain knowledge on how to create realistic plans, overcome obstacles, and set financial goals.

• It's also a great thing to make use of the tax-sheltered assets while you're still young through job incentive programs.

• You might also benefit from mastering essential financial skills, including earning, saving, spending, and assessing the state of the economy. Benefits of Finance Management.

When it comes to personal financial issues, a lot of college students depend on specific family members or parents for assistance, while some quickly waste student loans. Being able to save and manage money well is one benefit of having good financial management skills. This will enable you to have more money, which you may use for important things like projects.

Once you have mastered the art of managing your finances, there are still more things you may encounter. This might be your first step towards success if you wish to succeed in the future. Even if managing money is not an easy task, it can be done on a daily basis. The process of financial management is methodical. It will take time to complete this, especially if you don't mind spending money because you know you'll be able to pay off your debts once you obtain employment. Asking your friends or anybody you know for advice if you struggle with money management may also be beneficial.

Section I

SETTING UP YOUR NEEDS

Setting limits is the first step towards improving your life when it comes time to do so. This is beneficial for both your personal and professional lives. No matter how big or small the project is, it doesn't matter. The key to your prosperity is understanding where to start, how to organize it, and what matters most.

Make a list of everything you need to do.

You need to know what you are doing at any given moment during the day when you have activities. Listing all the errands you intend to run on any given day is a great approach to figuring out how to organize each task and ensure that it is completed correctly. Think of this as a lot like Marie Kondo's method for organizing your space. Before you organize and arrange it, you ought to be able to view everything you have.

Place Every Task in the Appropriate Group

Try to assign each task to a class that indicates its purpose, such as work or person. Determine whether this assignment is important, urgent, or something else at that point. This can help you identify tasks that you can delegate to someone else to complete and identify errands that you are running that you can just stop.

Put Critical Tasks First

When you realize that some of the tasks are important, move them to the top of the list. Some find it helpful to separate work from personal life, while others prefer to simply make a list of errands and the order in which they will be completed. You have the option to create two records or combine everything into one, provided that you have correctly identified the situation— whether dire or not.

Determine the Task's Value

It's worth it, and it's something you should look at for every task. If it turns out to be a job issue, this is easier to identify. You understand that having an item that others can buy available for purchase will bring in money, so it is highly valuable. Nevertheless, you also understand how crucial it is to get your child to her piano lesson.

Recognize the Work That Will Be Needed

While you are organizing your projects, keep in mind this additional important point. It is also useful for evaluating effort in relation to value in order to help define an undertaking. How much time does anything really need to take you to complete? What is the cost of your reevaluation in money? Sort through all the resources that each task requires be it money, resources, or a tool that makes the task easier (for example, maybe you need to buy expensive and hard-to-understand software to complete this task). In the last example, after focusing on the situation, you may choose to, for example, reclaim.

Determine Which Tasks Should Be Outsourced or Cut

Now that everything is in the open, it's important to look over the tasks and determine which ones you can delegate to someone else or which ones you really do not need to complete yourself. The important thing is to give up the things you don't have to do yourself when it makes sense to do so, whether it's cleaning your house, making dinner, doing your clothes, or, if you have a business, reappropriating something at work or in your enterprise.

When it comes to improving your life, try not to skip this step. If necessary, you can isolate it and complete individual, independent tasks.

Nevertheless, for a large number of individuals in today's world, work and life are inextricably linked, whether we like it or not. Understanding

what to concentrate on at work and home will greatly improve your clarity of life.
..Day ten

W
Would you prefer a summary of your financial status, a means of determining the true state of your money, or an idea of how you are doing month over month?
Then, becoming aware of your net worth is a fantastic and reasonably simple method to do this. Your net worth immediately reveals the state of your finances, including whether or not your balance sheet is generally favorable. It also provides you with a simple approach to creating goals, tracking improvements in your circumstances month over month, and obtaining a general understanding of the connections between the different aspects of your financial health.
In a nutshell, your net worth indicates your potential financial status if you sold everything you had and paid off all of your debts. It can be positive or negative. If your net worth is greater than your debt, you should still have money in reserve. In contrast, if your net worth is negative, you have more debts than assets, which means that even if you sold everything you owned, you still wouldn't be able to pay off all of your bills.
Like most people embarking on a financial journey, you will almost certainly be starting from a position of negative net worth. And by negative, I don't mean -$2,000, but probably closer to tens

of thousands of negative dollars, particularly if you have a sizable student debt or mortgage that you haven't paid down much of yet.

Such a figure should not depress you; rather, it should inspire you to change it for the better. After you've computed your net worth for the first time, it will be simple to continue doing so on a monthly basis, so receiving a summary each month will be straightforward and beneficial to keep you focused.

Part Two: What's the Point?

A popular saying says, "I don't mind buying; I just don't like being sold." For many online shoppers, this saying accurately captures their sentiments. There is a buyer for every price range if you, the seller, can convince the customer that he will receive at least twice his money back from the purchase he makes at your store. Customers don't mind buying more or even expensive items if they feel they are getting more value than they are giving up.

Therefore, we might argue that the value a product will provide to a buyer is more important than its price.

Therefore, the key is to keep in mind that customers always expect more than they are prepared to provide in terms of value—it doesn't matter if you sell inexpensive or costly goods. Recall that you must demonstrate to them in no uncertain terms the greater worth of what you are offering in exchange for the money. It's the age-old contrast between benefits and value. A product's features are its abilities, but their advantages are what they can accomplish for the customer. By clearly outlining the benefits that the customer, you should draw their attention.

I assure you that modern online customers are dubious. They have even lost money as a result of the various con games and frauds they have witnessed. Because they are so skeptical, today's online shoppers need to know exactly what the product will do for them before they would willingly enter their credit card information on your website. In essence, CREATE TRUST. Additionally, the qualities that the product offers and the price that customers are required to pay must make sense. This formula is easy to use. Should there be a significant disparity between the two, purchasers may become skeptical. If the price is too high, they might assume you're trying to con them, or if it's too low, they might assume there's a trick involved. You can't hold them solely responsible because a lot of Internet marketers utilize various dishonest and fraudulent tactics to entice customers to click the "Buy Now" button and engage in unethical business. DISREGARD THIS AT ALL RISKS.

You and your company will benefit when you've already made the essential decision to stand out from the crowd.

How to assist your clients in appreciating the worth of your offering and developing faith in your company

Inform the buyer of the true worth of your offering. This is what we have been talking about up to this point. To get the buyer to identify your product with those benefits, you must repeatedly highlight the advantages of your offering through advertising. Make use of every channel at your disposal: TikTok commercials, Facebook ad campaigns, Google ads, and affiliate ads can all be beneficial. Here, you want your product to be identical to the advantages that it provides to users. Always keep in mind that you want your product to always come to mind when a customer has a certain problem and that it is the best or only answer available.

Make a statement. Many of the products that compete with yours on online marketplaces like Amazon, eBay, and others are nearly identical to one another. How can you distinguish your goods from the competition? You must, however, learn something about your product that has never been done before, is original, or has only ever been seen online. People are eager to try the newest, hottest product on the market. Older models of anything—cars, drones, cell phones, etc.—are not appealing to anyone anymore. Keep in mind that consumers do not desire mediocre, out-of-date, or identical products that are readily available everywhere. They want the newest products to show off to their friends, create a reel, and boast about how amazing the price they found on your website was. This is a tendency that you should be aware of and market towards. Don't be subtle if you feel like you should be. When marketing your product, be brave and upfront; don't sugarcoat its advantages. Make sure the consumer understands what sets you apart from the many similar-seeming products that the competition offers.

Give a guarantee together with the merchandise. It may surprise you to learn that offering a guarantee along with your goods is the finest way to gain your audience's trust. Some con artists will indeed post a "Satisfaction Guaranteed" graphic on their website. Still, they have absolutely no intention of returning a customer's money or even responding to an unhappy customer's email. If we have previously established that you are devoted to becoming a different kind of internet marketer, offering a money-back guarantee reassures customers when they shop on your website. The most important thing is to convince the customer that you stand behind your product and will assist them if something goes wrong. If you're unsure whether to offer a full money-back guarantee, then always think about offering a free trial version of your product with an expiration date, a basic model with an option to upgrade to a premium model later if the buyer is satisfied, or go the traditional route and provide samples or a taste of your product.

The best policy is to be honest. I really don't know how else to put it, but. It is a fact that every salesperson is dedicated to emphasizing the positive aspects of the product and downplaying its negative aspects. This is acceptable up till you are being authentic about your offer or product. You are not being asked to lie.

First and foremost, you have to be confident in the worth of your offering and able to explain it to the customer in an understandable manner. There are a tonne of websites that sprout overnight, offer all kinds of promises, and then vanish from the internet scene without giving their clients any guidance. Recall that one of the finest rules for this area of your business is the traditional golden rule: be honest and treat others the way you want to be treated. Additionally, keep in mind that individuals discuss their experiences on your website in an open manner when they communicate online. You must take every precaution to keep those internet forums from damaging your reputation. The last thing you want is for one of your potential customers to read blog postings or forum comments that disparage your product. I can't emphasize this enough:

- Be truthful about what your product can and cannot accomplish.
- Be proud of it.
- Be honest about its capabilities.

Magnify, but don't deceive. Being sincere and lowering the bar may cost you some sales in the near run, but in the long run, your company will be built on a more stable foundation of honesty, and happy customers will frequent your website.

The Quantity Of Loan Requests

Finally, your credit score is somewhat impacted by the quantity of credit applications you have made. Your credit score drops a little each time you ask for a loan or even a credit card, even if it hasn't been accepted yet.

Financial organizations may be extremely vulnerable to customers who open multiple credit accounts quickly, particularly if they don't have a long credit history. This explains why many people notice a drop in their credit score when they get authorized for a certain loan or when they open a credit card. But the downturn is only momentary.

Remember that credit checks differ as well. It's interesting to note that if you check your credit, only a hard query will lower your credit score. I shall distinguish between soft and hard questions in the sections that follow.

When a loan application is sent to a lender, a hard inquiry is made. This could apply to a home, auto, or school loan. These queries impact your credit score.

In contrast, a soft inquiry is generated when you utilize your credit for a credit monitoring service, apply for a job, or get a copy of your credit report. There is no effect these kinds of inquiries have on your credit score.

How Is It Precisely Calculated?

Knowing that these elements don't have a set proportion is just as crucial as knowing how to compute your credit score. Because of the financial data gleaned from your credit report, they can differ.

This suggests that a person may make reckless judgments in an attempt to raise his credit score if he has a sufficient understanding of the fundamental elements mentioned above. Therefore, it is crucial to understand these elements.

Even while these are taken into account when creating a credit report, each person's credit report will weigh these elements differently.

Without recognizing the report as a whole, it is impossible to document how each element affects the credit score.

How to Look Up Your Credit Rating

You may check your credit score for free or very little money with certain services. should exercise caution and only utilize services you are familiar with. Several of these trustworthy services are free, particularly the ones that are mentioned below.

Section I

ESTABLISHING A DAILY PROGRAMMES.

Your morning routine usually serves as a blueprint for the rest of the day. A poor morning routine can realistically and mentally ruin your day. By establishing a positive tone for the day, our morning routine helps us better manage our schedules rather than having our schedules dominate us. We can better concentrate on what's in front of us, decide where to spend our time, and ultimately become more productive when we begin each day with a clean slate.

Establishing a morning routine is not about outperforming others or crossing more things off a list. Rather, it is about permitting oneself to start your day with self-assurance, serenity, and optimism.

Early mornings; the force of dawn.

A practice as transformative as rising early can affect our days and, ultimately, our lives in ways we cannot even begin to fathom. There is a sense of peace and tranquility because it is still early in the morning. The quiet solitude of the morning creates a hallowed space for contemplation, self-examination, and intention-setting. We can better organize our days, set realistic goals, and spend this priceless time doing things that are good for our bodies and minds. The secret to rising early is to take advantage of these quiet times and use them to discipline ourselves, become more productive, and give our days direction and energy.

A proactive attitude throughout the day is also established by rising early, which empowers us. It provides the priceless gift of "extra time"—a period for self-care and self-investment. By rising early, we make time for things like reading, exercising, eating well, and engaging in personal hobbies—things that are frequently neglected during the day's rush. It gives us a head start, enabling a calm and progressive start to the day, giving us an advantage in time management, intelligent decision-making, and welcoming the day with energy and excitement. The secret to the power of mornings is to give ourselves the gifts of time, intention, and a proactive outlook, which helps us set the stage for a productive and happy day.

Creating an Effective Morning Routine

Creating a morning routine that suits you requires planning a sequence of deliberate actions that prioritize self-care, establish a positive tone for the day, and support your goals. Let's examine a thorough guide that will help you create a morning routine that works for your needs and lifestyle.

- Recognise Your Priorities and Objectives:

We don't always know what we want to do that day, but occasionally we do. To begin, decide what your morning goals are. What are your career and personal objectives? Which things— exercise, mindfulness, education, or a particular hobby—do you prioritize? You can better organize your routine if you know what your goals are.

- What Is Your Allotted Time?

Determine the amount of time you can actually devote to your morning routine. Take into account your commute, other obligations, and your work or education schedule. You should ideally have a peaceful start to the day with your morning routine, so allow enough time for a leisurely and concentrated morning.

- Examine Your Personality Type:

Knowing if you are an evening (evening chronotype), morning (morning chronotype), or somewhere in between (intermediate chronotype) is crucial. Create your morning routine based on your preferences and innate energy levels. It works best during your most productive period of the day.

- Establish a Modest Schedule:

Make a general timetable that allows time for different tasks. Allowing for some flexibility is important since rigidity might backfire. Your daily routine should make you feel better, not worse.

- Include Important Components:

A decent morning routine requires a few things. Let's examine a few of them.

- Mindfulness and Reflection: To start in a positive frame of mind, take a moment to practice mindfulness, gratitude, or happiness.

- Physical Activity: To keep your mind and senses as keen as possible, incorporate stretching, yoga, exercise, or a morning jog or walk. Everybody needs something to totally remove their drowsiness. Yes?

- Nutritious Diet: A satisfying breakfast is the best. It is the meal of the day that is most significant. To prepare your body and mind for the next day, prepare a healthy breakfast.

- Personal Growth: To keep your mind active and promote growth, set aside time for reading, learning, or working on personal projects.

- Sip water to stay hydrated and focused. After going to bed, have a glass of water to rehydrate.

- Make self-care a priority. Make sure your daily regimen consists of self-care tasks like grooming, skincare, and any other activities that boost your self-esteem. Self-assurance is a beneficial and significant boost.

- Experiment and Make Adjustments: Start with a simple regimen and make adjustments to determine what suits you the best. Observe your feelings following each task. Adapt the order, length, or kind of activities to your requirements and interests.

- Track Your Development: How are things going for you? Assess your day's influence from your morning ritual on a regular basis. Do you feel more content, productive, or energized now? Over time, make use of these insights to hone and enhance your routine.

- Remain Devoted: Dedication is essential. To make your morning routine a habit, follow it religiously for a fair amount of time. To experience the long-term advantages, consistency is essential.

- Be Kind to Yourself: Recognise that not every morning will go as planned, and try not to be too hard on yourself. Be kind to yourself if you miss an activity or experience interruptions. The following day, start anew and keep improving your regimen.

Recall that the objective is to establish a morning routine that improves your general well-being, supports. It serves as your compass to help you go through the day with vigor and purpose.

Tricks Nos. 31–35

31. Look for Methods to Reduce Costs

Every cent saved is a penny earned, and this includes making little cuts to the costs you deal with on a daily basis. In the winter, reduce the heat by 2 degrees, and in the summer, increase it by 2 degrees. This will contribute to energy savings. Give up routines like stopping for coffee on the way to work. This contributes to increasing debt.

32- Examine Your Insurance Policy

Regardless, insurance is something we all need. Review your insurance with time. Examine the coverage for your car and home insurance. Because you are doing business with the same company, are you getting discounts? If you insure your home, car, and life with one insurance company, many of them will give you a discount.

33. Concentration and Focus Pay Off Financially

Your financial situation will also be affected if you tend to act and think erratically. Learn to regulate your thoughts and behaviors by keeping your attention on the work at hand, as opposed to accepting these as the standard. Reaching your goals and finishing a task faster than if you are disorganized is possible when you focus on one item at a time.

34. Become and Remain Organised

Keeping your financial affairs organized will help you stay on the path to financial independence. All of your receipts, bills, and costs should be kept in an expanding folder or filing cabinet. An online program can also help you stay up to date, but it's definitely best to do both. You can stay ahead of schedule if you set aside a few minutes every day to keep organized.

35. Make a Retirement Plan

Retirement has to be among your long-term objectives. You must choose the age at which you hope to retire and the kind of lifestyle you wish to lead at that point. Once you get your debt under control, you may begin making plans for this right now. Discuss your strategy for paying taxes now and in the future with a financial expert.

Chapter 3: Poverty Remedies

Being poor is an experience that nobody wants to have. Nope! However, poverty is a sly visitor who won't go away unless you take action to put an end to it.

Therefore, welcome to poverty if you've reached the point where your income no longer corresponds with your desires as expressed by your brain.

And now is the moment to manage your finances if you're sick and tired of living in poverty! You can find a way to stop being frugal, regardless of whether you need to work on your spending patterns, learn how to save money or find ways to earn more

bankrupt.

1. Learn to live below your means

Spending beyond what you earn will only create a road of debt behind you. You're not doing yourself any favors if you're living over your means in order to maintain your social circle or prove to others that you can support a certain way of life. Stop focusing on what others can afford and focus on how you can live within your means.

Put your credit or debit card away. They make it easier to spend money you don't need to spend. Change your thinking on consumption products.seeing dazzling TV programs that fuel your fantasies of buying. Learn to live below your means. That way, you'll have something left at the end of each month.

2. Develop a skill

You are typically broke either because you are unemployed (not earning), you don't earn enough or because you spend more than you make. There are three money skills you need to learn: money producing, money keeping, and money expanding abilities.

You can't maintain or increase the money you don't have. So, the most essential thing to do to quit being broke is to strengthen your money-earning talents. And what better way than to have abilities people are eager to pay for?

People don't generally have the money issue. What they typically have is a talent issue. If you have abilities others are seeking, they will pay money to obtain them.

So, if you want to quit being broke, start cultivating new talent. If you love to write, increase your writing abilities. If you adore logical thinking, you may try your hand at coding if you love art, study design, video production, graphics, and photography. There are various abilities you can develop. Just go and obtain self-education.

3. If you already have talent, become better at it

If you already have a marketable expertise yet are still poor, it's either your skill is not excellent enough for others to pay for it, or your marketing abilities require improvement. Make use of digital media to reach more prospects. If you are offering a product or service, consider ways of advertising. Learn social media and content marketing. And utilize this talent to market what you do.

4. Only give money you can afford to lose

Raise your hand if you have had a horrible experience lending money to someone close to you. You end up losing your money or perhaps ruining a friendship. I'm sure a lot of you can relate to this.

It's acceptable to provide a helping hand to someone in need. But that should be when you can afford to. If you are still fighting to find your feet financially, lending money you cannot afford to lose, which places you at the mercy of the borrower. To be on the safer side, only lend money you can afford to let go in the worst scenario.

5. Use the 50/30/20 rule

Senator Elizabeth Warren popularised the so-called' 50/20/30 budget rule' in her book All Your Worth: The Ultimate Lifetime Money Plan. The premise behind this guideline for budgeting is that 50 percent of your net income should go toward "needs," 30 percent should go toward "wants," and the remaining 20 percent should go into savings.

"Needs" would include items like food, prescriptions, rent, and insurance.

Some examples of "wants" include Netflix, cable, and manicures.

You may not necessarily reach the precise figures, but strive towards dividing your profits around that %.

To make this more successful:

Seek to pay yourself first.

Set away your 20 percent savings before any other expenditure.

Once you've depleted money for the month, let every trivial item wait until next month.

6. Stop purchasing on impulse

Instant pleasure is leading you into problems time and time again. There are numerous ways to spend money but fewer methods to make them. A key step to putting your finances in order is to instruct your money where to go instead of wondering where it went.

We have established that budget puts you back in the driver's seat, so you're no longer at the mercy of impulsive spending. If your possible buy isn't in the budget, slow down and back away. Remember that making little sacrifices today will pay dividends in the long term. Know what your final objective is, and then go for it!

If you constantly have a strategy for what you will purchase, you will have a much simpler time managing your funds. Your drive to acquire useless stuff will likely wane off after many days or perhaps a few hours.

Instead, prepare for every large expenditure. Save towards it. And make the choice deliberately.

To Display A Few Of Those.

1. Establish a speculative portfolio - Putting money into the stock market, exchange, common stocks, gold, or anything else that brightens your day is very important. Contributing is essential and maybe the easiest way to develop an optional cash stream. Not only will the project increase your basic wage and spark your curiosity, but the developing chief might also come in handy on a windy day (or weeks or months) when you've tragically lost your job or experienced a personal emergency. (Continued from Unit IV)

2. Begin outsourcing - Over the past ten years, the outsourcing industry has grown tremendously. All you really need to know is a little SEO, and a cursory look at the current exchange opportunities might turn you into the next multimillionaire. Now, let's face it: if you're not a multimillionaire, this will at least provide you with a starting point and some

breathing room in terms of reinforcement for your salary. Outsourcing has produced a great deal of them, and there will be many more in the future. Would you like to try the same?

3. SEO and the complete web setup - Building on the previous idea about SEO, you can actually put up an entire electronic setup where you can make money by renting out advertising spaces on websites. In any case, publicity will be the biggest thing for years to come, so if you believe the opportunity is gone, you're wrong, old friend, very wrong. 4. Create a blog or YouTube channel – Take the leap, believe in yourself, complete whatever task you have 100% of the time to complete, learn anything you can about the essence of the planet (if you are interested in it), and start writing a blog on the subject or, if you're not too shy to face the camera, create a YouTube channel. To be honest, I don't really understand this space that much. Initially, there may be a chance for it to

take off, and it may not succeed at all. Nevertheless, you will essentially feel satisfied that you tried your hand at something new. In the unlikely event that you consider the possibility that you're essentially doing something you don't enjoy at your current job, why not try your hand at a side project you enjoy and fail at it? The disappointment itself will reveal far more about you and your life than your job can. If it succeeds, even slightly, it will generate a commercial and transient revenue of roughly \$100–\$150, or ₹7,000–10,000 in happy cash. As a side gig, I don't think that is bad at all.

5. Rental revenue - Purchasing real estate and renting it out is a time-tested method of boosting your income. You may have to pay back a portion of the loan during the first few years out of your pocket, but once the loan is repaid, you will keep all of the rent plus the appreciation on the property, which is also

considered a return on investment. Now, there is a subject that tends to spark debates: What kind of real estate should I purchase? Where can I purchase it? Which portion should I enter, etc? My opinion is simple: invest money in a location you are familiar with and where you have backup plans for property maintenance in case you are unable to do so, preferably in your hometown. Sort of property to purchase? Any day, I would rather purchase an independent plot than a flat, mostly for independence and potential for wealth growth. I'll give you a call on whether to buy a commercial or residential type.

Again, these are just a few ideas you might think about and perhaps start earning some extra cash. Along these lines, as you could expect, you might receive ideas that are better suitable for you. Businesspeople aren't always born with different brains; what matters is their mindset, and an outlook is just a collection of different viewpoints. As you start looking into more contemporary viewpoints, you'll start to notice gaps and spaces waiting for you to fill them and earn some quick cash as an afterthought. Not only may you make quick cash, but you may also be able to transition from a side gig to full-time employment. If things go well, you might even become someone people look up to as their boss and grow your company much faster.

From a functional standpoint, you would need to work less if your firm grows and you hire more people to work for you. I'm not suggesting that you would contribute less to the company. I'm trying to say that you should make important decisions instead of randomly taking up things that could take a person 50–100 minutes to complete. That's also the main goal of developing automatic revenue streams.

Credits could be the answer to a good deal of your questions about augmentation, better working, enhancing, and entering flat or vertical expansion. Once money starts coming in, earning more money from present cash is a really straightforward task.

Chapter 2 of the Personal Finance Budgeting and Management Guide is 2.0. The Economic Crisis

You may have read online that "Money is not everything." It's said that having a large money account can buy you a Rolls-Royce and a Rolex, but it can't buy you the time you want to spend with your loved ones.

Just one more line will reveal that only those who have truly attained financial success say such things, so keep an eye out for them the next time you come across such a blog or article.

One of the benefits of financial prosperity is a greater sense of duty to your family. You gain the ability to help those in need as well as yourself. You enjoy stability and a certain measure of credibility and authenticity when you are financially independent. People also begin to regard you as an authoritative figure.

Furthermore, no! We do not advocate grouping individuals according to their ability to pay. Even so, having a healthy bank account might help you live a carefree life and accomplish your goals. Some people have it easy from birth, while others have to work hard to get to the top. Make sure you read this book if you are currently having financial difficulties. We've covered a few noteworthy strategies for pulling yourself out of the hole and leading the life you've always wanted.

Getting the basics right is essential. You will always be able to handle the challenging circumstances that come your way, thanks to your expertise and wisdom.

Handling Your Budget When Unexpected Bills Come In

To begin, budget $50 every week. After a year, you would have $2,600, exclusive of any interest, in case the refrigerator breaks down or malfunctions.

Experts advise searching for hidden funds by looking at your tax withholdings. If you receive a sizable refund each year, you might need to adjust your filing status in order to receive additional funds in your paycheck to contribute to an emergency fund. You are contributing your tax return funds to that fund, regardless of that.

Specifically, medical crises have the power to destroy a balanced budget completely. Negotiate significant medical expenses with the hospital, such as an emergency hospital stay. Nearly every hotel negotiates rates. The hospital or provider's office can often set up a payment plan if you get in touch with them right away rather than waiting until the amount goes into collections.

If not, you can combine all of your medical bills into one lower monthly charge by using an agency or a bank loan by using medical bill consolidation. This not only simplifies things for you, but the arrangement safeguards your credit score as you can make one-time payments. The drawback is that it can take you longer to pay off your debt in full.

Advantages If Budgeting

Controlling their finances transparently and proactively can be advantageous for all. Adhering to your budget can assist you in achieving a more favorable financial position.

Your life can be improved by budgeting because:

Delivers garbage. Making a budget sheds light on areas that many people overlook on a daily basis.

Sets priorities. A budget enables individuals to examine the overall picture of their spending patterns and establish new priorities to optimize their financial potential.

Forms new routines. People are able to shift expenditures into new categories and become more conscious of unnecessary spending when they have a clearer picture of how they have been using their money.

Minimize stress. Financing situations are among the most stressful situations. When there is a sense of control over the money coming in and going out, the strain can transform into an empowerment feeling.

Teaches. People can view money as a tool when they follow a budget, which shifts their perspective to prioritize long-term objectives and future requirements.

Making a budget is the first step; however, it's through budget maintenance that you will begin to realize true personal and financial progress. Adhering to a budget might provide a challenge for individuals who are not accustomed to setting financial boundaries or practicing self-discipline. Therefore, it is crucial to have a positive mindset toward the process.

Retaining motivation might assist in mitigating certain expenses associated with budgeting. Think about setting aside a small amount of money each month to look forward to a relaxing trip at the end of the year.

In the end, set realistic goals. Begin gradually and work your way up to a strategy that suits your lifestyle.

Best Ways to Save Money in Chapter Three

At any point, do you feel that finding practical money-saving advice is still challenging despite your best efforts? Even when you try to cut back on spending and have the best of intentions, something always comes up. Life throws a wrench in the works—the car needs new tires, the teenager needs help, the house needs a new roof—and just like that, saving money requires a second lounge. Does it sound familiar?

All of that magically organizing flawlessly before you start saving money is not necessary. It will never come if you wait around for the "perfect opportunity" to relocate. Right now is the perfect time to start saving money.

The good news is that there are many of easy ways to cut costs and add fresh funds and fresh air to your budget. These ten fantastic money-saving ideas will help you make adjustments to your expenditure and start saving immediately, putting you on the path to financial success.

Top 10 Money-Saving Advice: Put money aside. Furthermore, everyone has a different way of saving money, whether it's via delaying an exciting family outing or giving up that $4 mocha latte once a week.

Take advantage of these helpful money-saving tips to generate ideas on the best methods to save money in your daily life.

1. Pay Off Your Credit

In the unlikely event that you're trying to save money through preparation but are also anxious about a significant obligation, start with the obligation. Not convinced? When you factor in the time you spend reviewing your commitment each month, you'll quickly realize. The money that you are freed from having to pay interest on your obligation can easily be transferred into reserve funds. Among the options available to you for combining debts so you can handle them more easily is an individual credit extension.

2. State Your Savings Objectives

Imagining what you are saving money for is one of the best money-saving tricks there is. If you're feeling particularly motivated, consider setting savings goals and creating a schedule to help you save more easily. Need to pay a twenty percent down payment and buy a property in three years? You currently know what you need to save each month to reach your goal, and you have a goal in mind. Utilize the reserve cash for the region to add machines to reach your goal!

3. Put Yourself First.

Establish a recurring automatic payment from your bank statements to your investment account each pay period. Make sure you don't cheat yourself out of a sound long-term reserve money plan, even if it's $500 or $50 like clockwork.

4. Give Up Smoking

No, it's extremely hard to stop, but if you smoke a pack and a half every day, you can understand why you would need to set aside over $3,000 in savings if you were to stop. This is a remarkable decline since the mid-1960s — come on in and join the club!

Fifth, go on a "Staycation."

Even though the name may be fashionable, the concept is sound. Instead of spending thousands on airline tickets to another country, completely search on your terrace for no special reason and travel up close and personal. Look for short outings in your area if you are unable to drive the distance.

6. Invest to Save

Can we simply be objective for a change and say that since utility expenses only go down somewhat over time, you should weatherize your home today and take responsibility for it? Make an energy review request over the phone with your service provider, or locate a guaranteed project worker who can provide you with a comprehensive home energy proficiency survey. This will range from little improvements like caulking windows and doorways to installing new siding, insulation, or high-production ENERGY STAR appliances and machinery. Over time, you might save hundreds of dollars on power bills.

7. Energy Efficient

You can save three to five percent of your energy bills by lowering the indoor regulator on your water radiator by ten degrees. Adding a tankless or on-demand water radiator can also save up to 30% of investment dollars as compared to a traditional tank water warmer used for storing.

8. Get your lunch ready.

Finding regular reserve monies is an obvious strategy to conserve money. If eating lunch at work costs $7 while packing your lunch only costs $2, you may then build up a $1250 emergency fund.

9. Open an account that pays interest.

For most of us, separating your emergency savings from your bank statements reduces the likelihood that you may occasionally need to obtain investment cash. If your goals are longer-term, think about investing in products with higher rates of return, such as a Regions

CD or Regions Money Market, which are significantly better than investing funds.

10. Make Your Expenses Annual

Do you spend $20 a week on snacks from the office candy machine? That's $1,000 that you're cutting out of your annual budget for soda and snacks. Surprisingly, that tendency adds up to a sizable total.

Conserving For Financial Independence

Financial Freedom: What Is It?

Everyone describes themselves as free from the rat race in terms of their personal goals. For a large number of people, it means having the financial cushion (reserve funds, investments, and cash) to cover the expenses of a particular style of life, as well as retirement savings or the freedom to pursue any career without having to secure a certain salary.

Being free of the rat race typically means having enough cash on hand, investments, and reserve assets to cover the expenses of the kind of life we want for our families and ourselves. It means creating emergency savings that allow us to leave or pursue the career we want without feeling obligated to earn a certain amount of money each year. Being free from the rat race means that our money is working for us rather than the other way around.

In what ways might you become financially independent?

In order to become financially independent, you must fulfil your buyer responsibilities, create a safety net of reserve monies, and generate enough automatic earnings through money management or company ownership to cover your present and projected daily expenses.

We struggle with mounting debt, financial emergencies, excessive consumer spending, and other problems that prevent us from reaching our biggest financial objectives.

Everyone faces these challenges, but you may improve your financial health by addressing the twelve corresponding propensities that go along with them.

When your money starts making money, you'll be free of the never-ending cycle of work and play!

Principal problems

Establish financial and lifestyle goals, both big and small, and make plans to reach them.

Budget your resources so that you can pay for all you need; follow through on this plan; pay off your credit cards to avoid taking on more debt than necessary; and keep an eye on your credit.

your money well, keep up with charges and rules, encourage automated contributions through your company's retirement plan, and establish a hidden savings account.

Make sure to ask for or haggle for better offers, live within your means, and practice frugal living whenever possible.

Handle your resources wisely since assistance makes more sense than replacement; above all, take care of yourself and maintain your health.

Free Money or Plenty of Assets

Being free from the rat race is having enough money to cover your daily expenses and enable you to afford many of your life's goals without working or, in any event, devoting any of your time or efforts to earning money. These resources may include one or both of the add-ons.

PART SIX: GROWING YOUR PROFIT

The primary cause of financial troubles, according to most people, is insufficient money to support their desired lifestyle. At the same time, financial gurus would always advise starting that saving habit with the little you have; this is okay in some circles but not in others. They characterize it as a postponement-based pursuit of financial independence.

In any case, you can need to hunt for more revenue streams in order to boost your income and, consequently, surpass the amount that is spent or, rather, lost.

As an employer under that corporation, you should first confirm that you are getting all the benefits to which you are entitled.If you belong to a union, you should be aware of the benefits to which you are entitled and that you are also receiving them. A person has the right to pursue reimbursement for any benefits they have been refused throughout their employment. This will enable you to get more money to help pay off your debts.

It might be necessary for you to look for several jobs which will allow you to raise your income significantly and assist in paying off your debts. It will be simpler to hunt for part-time work when compensation is based on the amount of hours worked. In this manner, you can work overtime on the weekends and on days when you're not working your full-time job.

You can also want to try your hand at side gigs, like selling supplements or providing delivery services, to get a taste of the sometimes highly lucrative world of entrepreneurship. Additionally, this will enable you to experience being your boss and might persuade you to quit your work.

Depending on how you feel about strangers poking around your home, you might try renting out some of the rooms. This is a good concept because you are making money off of something that is already yours. If you feel that it is invading your privacy, you can make sure that you have privacy by renting out your extra extension or the room next door.

Together with reviewing your compensation with your coworkers or the HR manager, you should make sure you aren't paying more than is necessary. It may turn out that you overstated your tax rate, in which case you might claim the additional funds you have been paying.

You may also choose to charge for the use of your skills; for example, you may offer piano lessons or even calligraphy and artwork to businesses that provide services. In order to sustain the network you build and, consequently, hope for a consistent or rising income that will help you in boosting your income, this will require your dedication, time, and networking abilities.

PART 7: GENERATE SOLUTIONS FOR PAYING YOUR DEBT

It makes sense that you come up with plans on how to repay these loans as quickly as possible so that regular life may return after you have previously evaluated the situation and determined how much money is owed and to whom.

Your financial adviser or debt advisor should work with you on this process as they have the knowledge and expertise to advise you on the best way to ensure that you pay back your debts as efficiently as possible.

This implies that you will figure out how to allocate your money such that the most important bills are paid off first, followed by the remaining debts in priority order. Your financial advisor will assist you in figuring out how to make sure you have enough money to get by for the rest of the month while still making your debt repayments.

You can choose to set aside a certain portion of your money on a monthly or sporadic basis to pay your creditors. In the long term, this will help you make a significant dent in your debt, even though it will only be a small sum.

As you embark on your journey to being debt-free, be sure to set attainable objectives that will sustain your motivation.

To start, you might include the deadline along with simple reminders of the bills you need to pay off. These reminders may appear in your calendar, on sticky notes placed on your wall or desk, or your cell phone. These will act as reminders for you to consistently pay your debts.

To avoid having to hunt for other sources of income, try to have a set quantity of cash in your purse at all times. This will limit your daily spending to a specific amount, and over time, it will become a helpful

Chapter 1: Overview

Hi there! You're likely going through some difficult financial circumstances if you're reading this. Remain calm; you are not by yourself. Unexpected obstacles are thrown at us in life, and occasionally, it feels like we're in a hurricane. The good news is that financial storms pass, and you can weather them and come out stronger if you have the correct strategies.

Present-Day Financial Environment

Let's start by closely examining the financial scene. Personal finances are impacted by the ups and downs of the economy, which can resemble a roller coaster. Perhaps you've been struggling to make ends meet due to an unexpected bill, a medical emergency, or a job loss. There are others besides you. Together, we'll ride out this financial turbulence.

Let's start with some sobering facts and true tales to set the scene. Gaining insight into the wider economic landscape might help you see how your journey fits into the bigger scheme. It helps you traverse the financial landscape like a map.

Financial Difficulties Examples

Narratives have great power. They help us feel connected, motivated and reassured that we are not struggling alone. In this chapter, we'll look at actual cases of people dealing with various financial difficulties. These true tales, which range from an abrupt job loss to unforeseen medical expenses, will strike a chord with you and demonstrate that anyone can experience financial hardships.

My goal in telling these experiences is to foster understanding and a sense of community. Financial difficulties are not unique to you, and there is a wealth of knowledge to be gained from individuals who have triumphant over comparable circumstances.

The Value of Speedy Resolutions

There is not much time left. Postponing action when experiencing financial challenges can make matters worse. We'll go into the reasons it's important to deal with financial concerns as soon as possible in this part. There are many advantages to acting quickly, including avoiding further debt buildup and protecting your mental health.

Consider it similar to tending to a wound. It will heal more quickly if you clean and bandage it right away. In a similar vein, prompt financial planning can hasten your recovery and give you back control over your financial destiny.

Summary of the Contents of the Book

Let's now discuss what this book has in store for us. Together, we are starting a trip, and my role is to lead you through the necessary, doable steps. We'll cover everything in the upcoming chapters, including evaluating your financial status, settling debts with creditors, looking into potential sources of income, and developing long-term financial resilience.

This book is a toolkit that will provide you with the knowledge and solutions you need to overcome financial obstacles, not just a list of rules. You will have the skills necessary to weather any financial storm at the end of this journey, with each chapter serving as a stepping stone toward financial stability.

So fasten your seatbelt! We're going to delve deeply into the realm of quick cures for money problems. It won't be simple, but I assure you it will be worthwhile. Together, we'll close this chapter of uncertain finances and begin a new one that is full of stability, resiliency, and financial security.

Putting Your Financial Situation In Focus

One of the most important steps to knowing your present financial condition is to create a Snapshot of Your Finances. This is how you do it:

1. Compile your financial records: Gather all pertinent financial records, such as bills, investment account statements.

2. record Your Income: Create an exhaustive record of all the money you receive on a regular basis, including your salary, rental income, revenue from freelancing, and any other sources of income.

3. Keep Track of Your Expenses: Sort and document your outlays throughout a predetermined time frame, usually a month. Add both variable and fixed spending (such as groceries, entertainment, and eating out) along with fixed expenses (such as rent or a mortgage).

4. Draft a Statement of Net Worth: Subtract all of your liabilities (debts) from all of your assets (savings, investments, property, etc.) to find your net worth. This number is an indication of your overall financial situation.

5. Establish Financial Goals: Establish both your immediate and long-term financial objectives. These could be accumulating money for a retirement.

6. Examine Your Spending Patterns: Go over your spending to find areas where you may make savings or more prudent financial decisions.

7. Verify Your Credit Score: Find out your credit score and ensure the authenticity of your credit report. Having a high credit score is necessary to be eligible for loans with affordable interest rates.

8. Examine Emergency Preparedness: In the event of unanticipated financial difficulties, make sure your emergency fund is sufficient to cover three to six months' worth of living expenses.

9. Review Investments: Check to see if your portfolio of investments matches your risk tolerance and long-term objectives. Think about adjusting and diversifying as needed.

10. Assess the Coverage of Insurance: Examine your insurance policies to make sure they offer enough coverage for your needs, including health, vehicle, house, and life insurance.

11. Determine Your Ratio of Debt to Income: you may find your debt-to-income ratio. This

ratio can be used to assess your debt management skills.

12. Establish a Budget: Make a budget based on your income and expenses so you may reach your financial objectives. Set aside money for debt payments, savings, and personal indulgences.